A MIGHTY PURPOSE

by Warren Wilder Towle

The Silver Arch rises silently above
    The National Green,
Enshrining in its graceful majesty
    The work of man.
This curving steel
    Brilliant in the sun,
Stirs man's mind
    With memories of those
Who came
    Thrusting their courageous spirit
Into the West.

The strength of this Mighty Purpose
    Locked to the soil in depth,
Stands solid, fearless,
    To face all nature's force,
Like those who braved
    The early unknown task,
Baring themselves
    To the hardness of those times.
We marvel at what is done today
    As we look into the sky
Viewing man's creation.

We salute his vintage
    Fashioned in daring,
    Skill and art.
And trust that men
    Who come to view this shape
May grasp and hold
    Its spirit,
Noble,
Bold,
    In sweeping graceful silence
    And discover in its form
The Symbol of a new born day
    A gateway to man: Peace.

A MIGHTY PURPOSE

by Warren Wilder Toule

The Silver Arch rises silently above
The National Green,
Enshrining in its graceful majesty
The work of man.
This curving steel
Brilliant in the sun,
Stirs man's mind
With memories of those
Who came
Thrusting their courageous spirit
Into the West.

The strength of this Mighty Purpose
Locked to the soil in depth,
Stands solid, fearless,
To face all nature's force,
Like those who braved
The early unknown task,
Baring themselves
To the hardness of those times.
We marvel at what is done today
As we look into the sky
Viewing man's creation.

We salute his vintage
Fashioned in daring,
Skill and art.
And trust that men
Who come to view this shape
May grasp and hold
Its spirit,
Noble,
Bold,
In sweeping graceful silence
And discover in its form
The Symbol of a new born day
A gateway to man: Peace.

INTRODUCTION

O n the banks of the Mississippi River at St. Louis stands a national monument unique in concept, bold in design and unexcelled in beauty. The slender but sturdy stainless steel legs of the Gateway Arch rise to form a colossal catenary curve 630 feet above the ground.

Ambitious building projects have been undertaken by people of every generation. On the lists of the world's great edifices, however, this memorial is outstanding. It is doubtful that the engineers of the "Seven Wonders of the Ancient World" could have built this arch, since its construction required all the sophisticated skills of modern science.

St. Louis & the Gateway

The Arch is by far the most conspicuous landmark on the St. Louis horizon. It gracefully towers high above the city's skyline. This majestic monument not only symbolizes the gateway to the West, but also commemorates the acquisition of the Louisiana Territory. It stands as a memorial to the epic story of the American pioneers, explorers, trappers, traders, gold-seekers, missionaries and soldiers who opened up the vast wilderness west of the Mississippi. Today, travelers are invited to pass by or through this gateway as they journey across the country.

Fittingly, 91 acres on the St. Louis riverfront — site of Pierre Laclede's 1764 trading post — were chosen for the Memorial. Laclede's isolated outpost became the entryway for explorers, fur traders, home-seeking pioneers, miners and soldiers passing westward. It was also a mighty emporium for the natural wealth they found in the West. St. Louis well deserved its title, Gateway to the West. In his book *American Fur Trade of the Far West, Vol. 1*, Hiram M. Chittenden aptly described St. Louis:

> *"It is doubtful if history affords the example of another city which has been the exclusive mart for so vast an extent of country as that which was tributary to St. Louis...Every route of trade or adventure to the remote regions of the West centered in St. Louis...Following the lines of trade, all travel to the Far West, whether for pleasure or for scientific research, all exploring expeditions, all military movements, all intercourse with the Indians, and even the enterprises of the missionaries in that country, made St. Louis their starting point and base of operations."*

It is this epic story of the nation's westward advance from the Mississippi to the Pacific Ocean that Jefferson National Expansion Memorial was created to commemorate and retell. St. Louis' proud role in that drama, as gateway to the West, is symbolized by the Memorial's towering Gateway Arch.

Opposite: The Gateway Arch towers high above the St. Louis skyline.

DREAMS OF A BOLD UNDERTAKING

*F*ounding fathers

The Memorial owes its existence to the vision and unrelenting determination of a group of St. Louis civic leaders known as the Jefferson National Expansion Memorial Association (JNEMA). If not for their efforts, this area might be nothing more today than it was when the Memorial idea was conceived — 40 blocks of old business buildings, largely untenanted and decaying.

Luther Ely Smith first suggested the idea to St. Louis' Mayor Bernard Dickmann in the fall of 1933. It was a bold thought in the depth of the Great Depression to tear out a large portion of downtown St. Louis for a memorial to Thomas Jefferson, the Louisiana Purchase and the opening of the trans-Mississippi West. Mr. Smith's idea drew an enthusiastic response from St. Louis civic leaders. In April 1934, Mr. Smith became chairman of JNEMA.

Federal commission appointed

Seeing the proposed memorial as a national undertaking, JNEMA planned a joint project. The federal government would aid the city by supplying two-thirds of the estimated $30 million required. First, the Association petitioned Congress to establish a United States Territorial Expansion Memorial Commission to plan the Memorial. A resolution was passed by Congress and signed by President Roosevelt on June 15, 1934. It set up a commission of three presidential appointees, three House of Representative appointees, three Senate appointees and six JNEMA appointees.

The commission's purpose was "to consider and formulate plans for the construction, on the western bank of the Mississippi River, at or near the site of Old Saint Louis, Missouri, of a permanent memorial to the men who made possible the territorial expansion of the United States, particularly President Thomas Jefferson and his aides, Livingston and Monroe, who negotiated the Louisiana Purchase, and to the great explorers, Lewis and Clark, and the hardy hunters, trappers, frontiersmen and pioneers and others who contributed to the territorial expansion and development of the United States of America."

Roosevelt signs executive order

Jefferson National Expansion Memorial was established by an executive order signed by President Franklin D. Roosevelt on December 21, 1935. The order designated the National Park Service as the executive agency to acquire and develop the Memorial, with an allocation of $6,750,000 of federal funds, to be matched by $2,250,000 from the city. On June 22, 1936, the National Park Service established an office in St. Louis for development of the Memorial.

Opposite: The bold design of the Gateway Arch makes it a fitting tribute to those who opened the West.

Luther Ely Smith   *Bernard F. Dickmann*

Land acquisition began in June 1937. Within 13 months, the government filed 40 petitions for land condemnation — one for each block within the proposed boundaries of the Memorial. Building demolition began on October 9, 1939. By the time it was complete in 1942, World War II had brought development to a halt. The cleared area became a temporary civic parking lot. Work resumed following the war.

Aerial view of the Memorial site in 1942, after the razing of business and industrial buildings.

The Old Courthouse

Due to its historical significance and architectural beauty, the Old Courthouse was added to the Memorial in May 1940, when President Roosevelt approved its acceptance from the City of St. Louis. Extensive restoration of the building enabled the National Park Service to establish headquarters there on December 1, 1941. Interpretive planning began soon after establishment of the Memorial, and exhibits were opened to the public in the Old Courthouse on October 20, 1942.

Architectural competition announced

The design for the Memorial resulted from the nationwide architectural competition which JNEMA sponsored in 1947. In a two-year campaign beginning in 1945, the Association raised $225,000. Offering five semi-final prizes of $10,000 each and a grand prize of $50,000, the competition drew 172 entries from leading American architects. The winner, announced on February 18, 1948, was Eero Saarinen, a young architect of Finnish descent.

Architect with a vision

Born in Finland in 1910, Eero Saarinen was the son of Eliel Saarinen, a noted and respected architect. His mother, Loja Saarinen, was a gifted sculptor, weaver, photographer and maker of architectural models. Eero Saarinen grew up in a household where drawing and painting were taken very seriously. He was instilled with a devotion to quality that would remain with him for the rest of his life. He was also taught that each object should be designed in its "next largest context — a chair in a room, a room in a house, a house in an environment, an environment in a city plan."

In 1923, the Saarinens emigrated to the United States and eventually settled in Michigan, north of Detroit. It was here that Eliel Saarinen established the Cranbrook Institute of Architecture and Design.

Between 1930-1934, Eero Saarinen formally studied at the Yale School of Architecture. After a two-year fellowship in Europe, he returned to Cranbrook in 1936 to become an instructor of design and his father's partner in the architectural firm. It was during this period that he began to build a reputation as an architect who refused to be restrained by any preconceived ideas. He maintained that the future must remain open to the exploration of new forms and principles, with the ultimate goal being the advancement of architecture as an art and a profession.

After working with his father on a number of projects, Eero Saarinen had a chance to express his philosophy when he entered the 1947 architectural competition for the Jefferson National Expansion Memorial. This was his first great opportunity to establish himself as an independent architect. He intended to create a monument not only to Thomas Jefferson and the nation, but also to the modern age. For him, "The major concern...was to create a monument which would have lasting significance and would be a landmark of our time...Neither an obelisk nor a rectangular box nor a dome seemed right on this site or for this purpose. But here, at the edge of the Mississippi River, a great arch did seem right."

Saarinen carefully studied the site and its surroundings to ensure that the design would encompass the whole environment and not just the monument. The arch was to rise majestically from a small forest set on the edge of the great river. It was considered perfect in its form and its symbolism.

The Arch was his first great triumph, but there would be many more for Eero Saarinen. Projects such as the General Motors Technical Center, the TWA Terminal in New York and the Dulles International Airport brought him more acclaim. They also helped establish him as one of the most successful and creative architects of his time. It was a well-deserved reputation. Throughout his career, Saarinen was guided by the basic belief that, regardless of the project, quality and originality were to be consistent features.

As his designs show, Saarinen was clearly a man of vision. Although his life was cut tragically short, his vision lives on through the structures he created. The Gateway Arch marked the beginning of his career just as the Gateway to the West marked the beginning for countless pioneers. In both cases, the desire was to move boldly toward the future. The Arch is ultimately a monument to all those with a vision, such as Thomas Jefferson, the pioneers and Eero Saarinen.

Eero Saarinen, winning architect in the design competition for the Memorial.

Ground breaking

Actual construction of the Memorial began on June 23, 1959, when ground-breaking ceremonies were held for relocation of the elevated railroad tracks that once passed over the Arch grounds. The second phase of construction, which began on February 11, 1961, involved excavation for the visitor center and the foundations of the Gateway Arch. This phase also entailed redevelopment of the levee along the east side of the Memorial. This work was completed late in 1963.

In March of 1962, a contract for nearly 11 1/2 million dollars was awarded to the MacDonald Construction Company of St. Louis to build the Gateway Arch and underground visitor center. Two months later, the National Park Service signed a cooperative agreement with the Bi-State Development Agency to coordinate the construction and operation of the Arch transportation system.

The concrete shell of the visitor center was substantially completed during 1962, and the first stainless steel section of the Arch was placed on the south leg on February 12, 1963. The section, an equilateral triangle 12 feet high and 54 feet on a side, weighed 101,500 pounds.

A unique challenge

When they undertook construction of the Arch, the MacDonald Construction Company and its subcontractor for the Arch shell, the Pittsburgh-Des Moines Steel Company (PDM), found themselves faced with a problem unique in building history. Nothing like the Arch had ever been constructed before. The intricate engineering calculations and the actual stainless steel construction were carried out by PDM, under the supervision of the National Park Service and Eero Saarinen Associates.

The Arch demanded extremely sophisticated engineering. A

CONSTI

deviation of any magnitude between the bases could result in the legs of the Arch failing to meet perfectly when they reached the top. Adding to the construction problems, extreme care had to be exercised to protect the gleaming surface of the stainless steel composing the outer skin.

Creative engineering

As plans progressed, the engineers proposed several schemes for hoisting the stainless steel sections. Among them was the building of tower structures 6 feet square and 700 feet tall supported by millions of feet of guy wires. This plan and others were ruled out as being too costly and impractical. The final solution was a creeper derrick, an 80-ton tilting platform. The platforms for the derricks were 43 feet by 32 feet. Each had its own tool shed, a heated shack for the workmen, sanitary facilities and communications equipment. These derricks were mounted on tracks fastened to the Arch itself and supported a stiff-legged derrick with a 100-foot boom. These rigs climbed the

UCTION

The Arch is constructed of double walls filled with steel-reinforced concrete and steel stiffeners.

Arch to sit at pre-determined stations. They then lifted the sections with the derrick and put them in place. Each time it was raised, the derrick had to be leveled to adjust to the changing curvature of the legs. The first six sections of each leg were placed with conventional cranes. Above this point, the creeper derricks were used.

Each of the 142 triangular sections of the Arch was constructed of double walls of steel. As the legs of the Arch went up independently, they were strengthened by pre-stressed steel rods embedded in concrete up to the 300-foot level. Above that height, steel stiffeners instead of concrete were used between the inner structural steel plates and the outer stainless steel plates.

The final section

One of the most interesting operations was that involved in placing the last section of the Arch. This occurred after the creeper derricks had climbed to the 610-foot level. By this time, workers were on a near horizontal plane. An 80-ton stabilizing strut was installed between the two legs at the 530-foot level to support them until they could be joined.

The lifting of the final section was scheduled for 10:00 a.m. on October 28, 1965, but started at 9:26 a.m. to avoid possible complications from the sun. The stainless steel of the south leg had begun to expand in the morning heat. Water was used to cool the leg of the Arch, but had only a temporary effect. The workers had to move quickly.

Before placement of the final piece, a gap only 2 feet wide remained. Jacks mounted on the top opened the gap to 8 feet by applying 500 tons of pressure. This allowed the last section to be inserted. When the pressure was released, the natural thrust of the legs clamped the section in place. Once it was welded, the jacks and stabilizer strut were removed. The creeper derricks then lowered themselves down the tracks. As they went down, the derrick tracking was removed, the bolt holes were repaired and the stainless steel surfaces were polished.

The completion of the outside of the Arch was celebrated on October 28, 1965. Work, however, continued inside and under the Arch. The underground visitor center, the Museum of Westward Expansion, the Tucker Theater and the transportation system that would carry visitors to the top still remained unfinished.

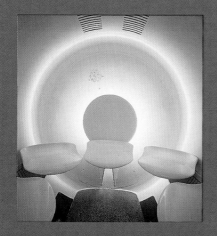

THE ARCH TRANSPORTATION SYSTEM

An elevator to the sky

The transportation system that would carry visitors to the top of the Arch offered the engineers many challenges, as well. Early proposals for the system were based on elevators. A standard elevator would have taken visitors to the 300-foot level for transfer to a smaller, steeper elevator. Six stories of the Arch would have been needed between the two elevators to allow for machine rooms and adequate waiting space for visitors. The elevator notion was determined to be impractical. Next, escalators were considered but were ruled out, as well. Another idea considered was a "Ferris wheel" design that would have run on a track up one leg, across the top, down the other leg and across the underground visitor center. The flaws of this design were that it required a track nearly one half mile in length and did not allow for adequate loading and unloading space at the top.

The plan that worked

The final design developed out of a combination of the Ferris wheel and elevator ideas, resulting in two independent trams of eight 5-passenger capsules, which climb a track up and down the legs of the Arch. The capsules consist of a 5-foot diameter barrel in a ring-and-trunnion framework. With the assistance of a small motor, the tilt of the capsule is corrected to maintain an upright position as the angle of the leg changes.

When the tram begins its journey skyward, the tracks are overhead. As it climbs and the angles in the legs change, the capsules pivot around the track. When the tram reaches its destination at the top, the tracks are underneath the capsules. The trip to the top takes 4 minutes, and the return trip only 3 minutes. At the top, visitors climb a short flight of steps to the observation room. The room is 65 feet long, 7 feet wide and can accommodate 100 people. Each of the 16 windows on a side offers a spectacular 30-mile panoramic view to the east or the west. During an average summer day, nearly 6,000 people may make the trip to the top!

Along with the tracks and capsules, other routes to the top were also being installed. There are two 12-passenger supplemental maintenance elevators that travel half-way up the legs, as well as a 1,076 step spiraling staircase. On July 24, 1967, the first visitor rode the north tram. Work, however, continued on the south tram for 8 more months. At last, the Arch was completed. On May 25, 1968, nearly 20 years after the Saarinen Arch won the competition, Vice President Hubert Humphrey addressed the dedication of this great monument as "a monument to a dream, a memorial to the time of the West."

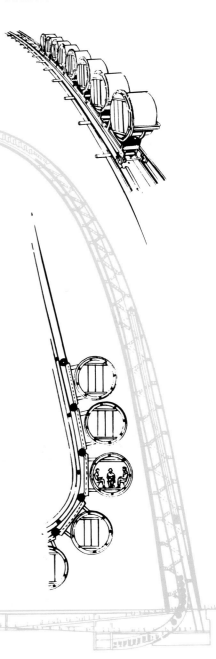

Opposite left: Passengers ride to the top in capsules, each seating five people.

Right: A tram of eight capsules climbs a track to its destination at the top of the Arch.

G A T E W A Y
ARCH

GATEWAY ARCH 630'

WASHINGTON
MONUMENT 555'

STATUE OF LIBERTY 305'

SCALE 1 INCH = 100 FEET

FACTS ABOUT THE ARCH

How big is it?

The Gateway Arch is one of the newest monuments within the National Park system. At 630 feet, it is certainly the tallest. Comparing it to two other well-known National Park features, the Arch is 75 feet higher than the Washington Monument and over twice as tall as the Statue of Liberty. Also, by way of comparison, the 60-foot heads carved on the face of Mount Rushmore are designed to the scale of men 465 feet tall, a height that could easily allow such giants to walk through the legs of the Arch. The Arch surpasses Egypt's Great Pyramid (450 feet) in height, but is smaller than the Eiffel Tower (984 feet). While the Gateway Arch is unmatched as a monument, several buildings, such as New York's Empire State Building (1,250 feet) and the World Trade Center (1,350 feet) or Chicago's Sears Tower (1,454 feet), would tower over the symbol of the Gateway to the West.

The Arch is what is known among engineers as an inverted, weighted catenary curve. A catenary curve is the shape assumed by a chain hanging freely between two points of support. "Inverted" means the curve is projected upward to form an arch. "Weighted" means that the lower sections of the legs are larger than the upper sections. In the catenary, the most structurally sound of all arches, the thrust passes through the legs and is absorbed in the foundation.

The Arch has a span between the two legs equal to its height, 630 feet. In cross section, each leg is a double steel-walled equilateral triangle, each side measuring 54 feet at the base and 17 feet at the top. The double walls are 3 feet apart at the bottom, diminishing to 7 5/8 inches in the upper sections, leaving a hollow core 48 feet wide at the base and tapering to 15 1/2 feet at the top.

The stainless steel panels on the outside of the Arch diminish in size as it goes up, from 6 x 18 feet to 4 x 5 2/3 feet, each 1/4 of an inch thick. To complete, the Arch required nearly 900 tons of stainless steel. The interior walls are composed of approximately 2,200 tons of 3/8-inch carbon steel plate with 1 3/4-inch plates at the corners.

Despite the Arch's great height and comparatively small size at the top, extreme wind pressures are hardly noticeable to visitors at the top. It is designed to withstand a wind load of 55 pounds per square foot, the equivalent of a 150 mile per hour wind. Even under this unlikely pressure, the Arch would sway only 18 inches in an east and west direction.

THE MUSEUM OF WESTWARD EXPANSION

*D*eveloping the museum

In the early days of planning for the Memorial, a large rectangular room next to the visitor center was reserved for a future museum. The floor space exceeded the area of a football field. Heavy concrete pillars supported the ground level ceiling. Like the rest of the visitor center, the museum would be entirely underground. The theme or title, "The Museum of Westward Expansion," was not a simple one. Within this single space, the entire story of America's century of westward expansion, 1800-1900, would be on display.

In 1970, responsibility for designing the museum went to a Washington, D.C. architectural firm, the Potomac Group. Under the direction of Aram Mardirosian, architects, historians, designers and artists developed a radically different kind of museum that opened in 1976. The original rectangular room was completely altered so that exhibits were displayed in a large, semi-circular area in a series of broad, wedge-shaped sections. Dates visible on rings on the ceiling divide these areas into 10-year periods. The sections detail aspects of life on the frontier such as mining, exploration, settlement, farming and Native American cultures. Ethnic, religious and racial groups that made the West a unique place are represented. The museum is unusual in that no exhibit labels are used. The story of the American westward experience is told through the objects, clothing, tools and words of the people who lived there.

Jefferson & the Louisiana Purchase

The museum begins with the year 1800, just outside the reach of the life-size bronze statue of Thomas Jefferson, America's third president. Jefferson's vision of a continental America was at the heart of the westward movement. In the opening years of the 19th century, Jefferson succeeded in buying the Louisiana Territory from France. The territory included all lands west of the Mississippi River and east of the Rocky Mountains. It cost the young nation 15 million dollars, about 5 cents an acre, and doubled the size of the country. With the middle third of the continent in American hands, the way was open for a drive to the Pacific.

Museum layout

That drive can be followed in the museum by moving toward the back wall. Each circular area contains exhibits from the decade it represents. Major themes of westward expansion take form through photographs, great paintings, quotations and actual objects, such as boots, hats, guns, knives, beads and tobacco.

Opposite: A life-size bronze statue of Thomas Jefferson stands at the entrance to the museum. Each ceiling ring represents an historic decade of westward expansion.

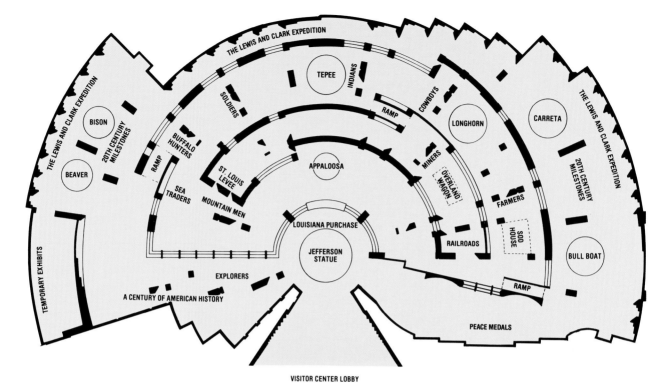

THE LEWIS AND CLARK EXPEDITION

VISITOR CENTER LOBBY

Through the pictures, quotations and objects, the museum becomes an archive. Through its organization, it becomes a computer. The museum, as a whole, is put together to show the way people lived, what they wore, what they ate, what they said and even the music they heard. The museum shows when people lived, how they lived and where they lived. Labels and descriptions are unnecessary as the exhibits suggest their own story. Each is designed to tell a part of America's western epic.

Lewis & Clark

Along the back wall are photographs of the American landscape as it appeared the day Lewis and Clark wrote of it in their diaries. The Lewis and Clark expedition did more than survey the lands bought with American tax dollars. They left their Wood River, Illinois camp in 1804, with instructions from Thomas Jefferson to observe, collect, measure and write about the unknown lands west of St. Louis. When they finally returned two years later, their official reports helped launch the first wave of Americans on history's greatest recorded migration.

The fur trade

The elegant hats worn by fashionable gentlemen in Europe and the eastern states were made with felt exquisitely coated with fine beaver fur. After Lewis and Clark's team returned from its successful penetration of the wilderness, the era of the fur trapper began. Lewis and Clark reported large numbers of beaver, enough to make more than

In 1804, Lewis and Clark left Wood River, Illinois, carrying hundreds of pounds of goods for trade with the Indians along the way.

one fortune. Fur trappers like Jim Bridger and Jedediah Smith became the famous pathfinders of the new country.

The fur trapper or mountain man display in the museum reveals more history than is at first apparent. One side is a large picture of a beaver. The tail touches inside the 1820s decade, while the nose pokes just short of 1845. The fur trade, although it begins earlier, became significant in the 1820s. By the 1840s, the yearly harvest of beaver pelts throughout the West was fast declining. About the same time, silk became popular in the hat industry, and the fur trade collapsed. On both sides of the column, pictures, paintings and quotations express something of the mind and attitude of the trapper. Between the sections of the column are the actual objects of life associated with the fur trade. A flintlock musket, a beaver trap, a skinning knife, a capote, or hooded coat made from a wool blanket, and a beaver hide stretched on a wooden hoop make up part of the typical kit carried by every successful mountain man. This one display expresses the object of the fur trade, the lifestyle of the trapper, his tools and possessions, his picture, his words and his time.

Meeting the Native Americans

Lewis and Clark were trespassers on lands occupied everywhere by Native Americans. For the most part, the mountain men reached a general understanding with the American Indian. Neither the Native Americans nor the mountain men threatened the vital interests of the other. Rather, there was much exchange between the two. In many ways, especially with the French traders, it was the white man who adopted the Native American way, not the other way around.

As fur trappers gained in experience and as their source of income became scarce, they became the guides for that second wave, the homesteader. The emigrant going west went with the intention of fencing, clearing and farming. They represented a direct threat to the American Indian way of life. The land would not support them both.

Trails west

The first trickle of emigrants began in the 1830s. These were men and women with no wealth except for their own labor. Everyone dreamed of paradise somewhere in a land called Oregon, or California. By the 1840s, the trickle was cutting through solid stone of the Rocky Mountains. Their ruts are still in the rock, as deep as any commandment. The covered wagon in the museum is typical of some used on the march west. Solidly made with a few nails, some wooden pegs and iron-rimmed wheels for good mileage, it was pulled by mules or oxen. Few wagons had seats. Most folks heading west walked the 2,000 miles to the "promised land." Within a few years, the Oregon Trail and California Cutoff were littered with the provisions of wagons too heavily loaded. The truth of the hard road convinced many that what seemed a necessity in the beginning was, after all, a luxury not worth

The overland wagon carried the possessions of thousands of travelers seeking a new life in the West.

the effort. If the burden was heavy on the white man, the next few decades would be crushing to the Native American.

Early in the 1600s, the American Indian of the Plains and Southwest found unexpected profit in stealing horses from Spanish outposts and, later, from each other. Within a few years, the American Indians of the Plains developed into one of the greatest horse people in the world. Mounted on his small swift horse, the Indian outrode and outfought the U.S. Army for nearly 50 years. The tribes broke only after the lands were scorched, the bison were gone and the villages were reduced. The coming of the white man ended a way of living centuries old.

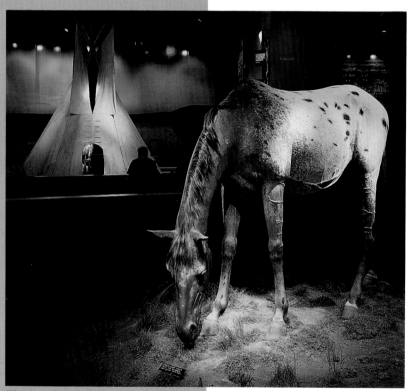

The American Indian tipi and the horse, such as the Appaloosa, were commonly recognized features of Plains Indian life.

American Indian peace medals
American Indian peace medals, produced in silver for presentation to Native American chiefs and warriors, represent fascinating and little-known aspects of American history. They also embody an important group of images depicting United States presidents, from George Washington to Benjamin Harrison. Peace medals were an integral part of the government's relations with Native Americans. Great care was taken in the production of the medals, and skilled die sinkers and sculptors were commissioned to create items of artistic merit. Indian Commissioner Thomas McKenney remarked that the medals were "intended, not for the Indians, only, but for posterity."

For Native Americans, the medals were cherished possessions to be worn on important occasions. The medals were buried with their owners or passed down through the generations as symbols of power and importance. A significant number of Native American chiefs wear their peace medals with obvious pride in portraits and studio photographs of the last century. Medals were given to chiefs on such important occasions as the signing of a treaty, a visit of important Native Americans to the national capitol, or a tour of the tribe's country by a federal official.

The American Indian tipi

The American Indian tipi in the museum is made of buffalo hides tanned with animal brains. The tipi is typical of a tribe originally called Sioux by early French traders. Most tribes simply called themselves, "The People." Inside, the Indian-mistress arranged the living quarters, paying attention to traditional detail. It was her responsibility to raise the tipi, and when the camp moved, to take it down. She made the bedding the way her husband preferred and placed his possessions exactly where he liked them.

The exhibit displayed inside the tipi and on the walk shows the intricate relationships and dependence on the living world of the Native American environment. Most obvious is the bison. From the tipi hide, to glue for making and mending their tools, the American Indian found the buffalo essential for life on the Plains.

Bison hunters

In the early 1800s, millions of American bison grazed the western prairies. When the herds moved, thunder rose from their hooves. By 1892, the last herds perished under the gun sights of buffalo hunters and sportsmen. In 1900, the last known herd was a group of about 39 animals roaming magnificently in Yellowstone National Park, unaware that their once uncountable companions were all but exterminated.

Standing on prairie pasture within the museum, a 1,700-pound bison symbolizes a West long since gone. His shaggy hair was prized by Native Americans for comfort against a long winter's night. They fashioned eating utensils out of the horns, thread from sinew, glue from hooves and meat from the muscle and fat. Nothing was wasted. Like an image on a Greek urn, the museum's buffalo reminds us of what once was, what still is, and what can never be again.

On a nearby column, the buffalo hunters are found in the 1870s. A buffalo rifle, a saddle, a knife and pictures of the important kill sites show the life of a hunter. Established near the outskirts of towns, the buffalo hunters' camps became important trade centers. One picture shows a pile of 40,000 hides waiting to be shipped to eastern markets. Buffalo tongues hang on racks to dry in the open air; the great carcasses have been left to rot in the hot Texas sun.

The annihilation of the great bison herds opened the vast prairies for livestock. Cattle, sheep and the cowboy multiplied upon the land. Despite the skill of the American Indian warrior, his way of life could not survive without the bountiful bison. Without a doubt, the buffalo hunter caused the American Indian the most lasting damage.

Each eagle feather added to this 1870's Sioux war bonnet represented a coup, a personal deed of bravery, by its owner.

After the Civil War, Texas Longhorn Steer became the substitute for the depleted beef supply in the East, which led to the long drive and the Cowboy Era in the West.

The U.S. Army provided the umbrella under which the hunters worked. For a foot soldier, life was more than bitter Plains warfare. Far from his home, there was little consolation for a loneliness as wide as the land. A few dated letters, a small picture of a dimly remembered wife and a harmonica were all there was. The American Indian's way of life was not the only one that changed.

New found wealth

During these busy years, it was normal to see San Francisco Bay filled with ships bound for foreign ports. In 1849, clipper ships lined the wharves, abandoned. The crews, like so many other adventurers, had left in haste for the gold fields of the famous Mother Lode, a golden El Dorado in the foothills of the Sierra Nevada. Most would come out with little to show except for a few used picks and shovels and a debt to the general store. Even those that struck the rich vein failed to make it a foundation of permanent wealth. Most of the riches ended up in the big banks and investment houses. Still, it was a great dream. Gold-feverish men piled into California by the thousands, then on to the Black Hills of Dakota, back again to Colorado and, finally, into the vast Yukon Territory for one last chance to get rich.

The gold miners' column in the museum is leafed with real gold. Attached are a gold pan, a pick and a shovel. The legendary burro is pictured above the possessions of a grizzled prospector. The picture of John Marshall, the man who made the first strike, does not show the glow of a man of wealth and fortune. Instead, it is a man haunted by his first famous discovery. He eventually came to believe he owned all the gold in California. In the end, Marshall was driven from the mining camps a broken, penniless man.

The country was captured mostly by men and women eager to begin a life of their own. Whether in the lush Willamette Valley of Oregon or in the former "great American desert" of eastern Colorado, Kansas, Nebraska and Oklahoma, these families formed the skeleton of society that fleshed out the new America. Standing again near the statue of Thomas Jefferson, the entire story of the West appears in one vast, sweeping vision. It almost seems possible to capture the entire history in this one view of the museum. To see the details or the reality, however, you must descend and approach each part separately. The complete vision becomes lost. Gone is the hope of seeing all the detail forming the larger truth that was the American West.

If there is a basic truth found in the museum, then it must be that history does not belong to the historian but to the way it really was. This museum attempts to show that way through the words of those who lived it, in the boots they wore, the world they saw and the land they paid for with the only currency they could respect.

This pilot's wheel, originally on a Civil War Ironclad, is typical of those that steered steamboats on the inland waterways.

THE OLD COURTHOUSE

St. Louis & the Old Courthouse

St. Louis was the true Gateway to the West during the 19th century, and its profile was accented by a tall, domed building in which many of the most important scenes of the city's life were played out. It was a public forum as well as a court-house. Slaves were auctioned from its steps in estate settlements, while one man's suit for his freedom helped plunge the country into Civil War. The history of the Old Courthouse mirrors the history of St. Louis and the entire United States.

The Old Courthouse stands on land donated to St. Louis County in 1816 by Auguste Chouteau and Judge John B.C. Lucas, to be "used forever as the site on which the Courthouse of the County of St. Louis should be erected." Up to that time, the courts had been housed in the Baptist church, a tavern and the commandant's house of the old Spanish fort. The first courthouse was built on the site between 1826-1828 in the federal-style. Within ten years, the city outgrew the building. A design by Henry Singleton was chosen for a four-winged structure with a low, classical dome in the center to be constructed of stone.

Cornerstone laid

Construction began on the existing courthouse on October 21, 1839, when the cornerstone was laid. Deposited in the cornerstone was a list of the officers of the general and state governments, a copy of different city newspapers and various coins. This phase of construction included only the west wing, the rotunda and two extensions from the rotunda that would later serve as links to the north and south wings. The federal-style courthouse of 1828 remained as part of the new building.

By 1843, the lower west courtroom was described as having fluted columns and massive railings around the bar, with a lofty ceiling. It was in this courtroom that one of the most important cases ever tried in the United States first came to the bar. In 1847 and again in 1850, an illiterate slave named Dred Scott sued for, and was granted, his freedom. Appeals to higher courts by his owner took that freedom away and led to the momentous Supreme Court decision of 1857, which upheld the ruling that Dred Scott should remain a slave, and declared the Missouri Compromise of 1820 unconstitutional. The Dred Scott decision hastened the start of the Civil War.

Opposite: The Old Courthouse and Gateway Arch form the Jefferson National Expansion Memorial.

Dred Scott began his fight for freedom in the Old Courthouse. His case resulted in a U.S. Supreme Court decision that helped spark the Civil War.

Rotunda design

The interior of the rotunda in the Old Courthouse was designed by George Barnett and completed near the end of 1844. Oak columns supported the upper galleries, and oil lamps were used for lighting. The official opening of the rotunda was held on February 22, 1845, when hundreds of people converged on the courthouse to hear the oratory of Uriel Wright. During this period, the rotunda functioned as a public forum, witnessing lectures, meetings, assemblies and other gatherings.

Emigrants bound for Oregon rendezvoused and organized at the Old Courthouse. Rallies were held for volunteers when the War with Mexico began, and troops were quartered in the rotunda. In October and November of 1846, anti-abolitionist meetings were held by slave owners "to devise ways and means to protect their slave property."

Asa Whitney spoke to businessmen in the rotunda that year, and meetings were held for the relief of famine victims in Ireland. Several important railroad meetings were held in the rotunda, including a national convention in October of 1849, at which Senator Thomas Hart Benton made an impassioned oration advocating a transcontinental railway.

The interior of the dome is decorated with historical murals by Carl Wimar and allegorical figures by Ettore Miragoli.

Construction continues

The second stage of construction of the Old Courthouse, planned by Robert S. Mitchell, began in 1851. The original brick courthouse of 1828, still standing on the east side of the building, was demolished. Between 1855 and 1860, the west wing was extensively remodeled, splitting the lower courtroom in which the Dred Scott case had been heard with a hallway. The old classical revival dome was removed because it now looked out of proportion with the expanded building. William Rumbold designed a new cast-iron dome in the Italian-Renaissance style, modeled after St. Peter's Basilica in Rome. Rumbold's iron dome, along with that on the federal Capitol in Washington, D.C., were among the first of their kind in the world. August Becker and Carl Wimar were hired to fresco the interior of the rotunda with historical scenes and allegorical figures. By 1862, the Old Courthouse looked much as it does today.

During the Civil War, meetings were held in the Old Courthouse to recruit soldiers, and special ceremonies took place in 1865 to honor President Lincoln after his tragic assassination. One of the last large events to be hosted was a reception for President Grover Cleveland in 1887. In 1930, the Old Courthouse ceased its official functions. In 1940, the building was deeded to the federal government by the City of St. Louis, and the National Park Service began restoration. The Old Courthouse became National Park Service headquarters for the Jefferson National Expansion Memorial on December 1, 1941.

The west courtroom, second floor, is restored to its 1860 appearance. The bench, railing and other furnishings, except for tables and chairs, are original.

The Old Courthouse today

The Old Courthouse, only two blocks from the Gateway Arch, today contains restored courtrooms, museum exhibits on local and national history, the splendid architecture of the building itself, Works Progress Administration dioramas and the headquarters of the Jefferson National Expansion Memorial. A film, "Gateway to the West," traces the history of St. Louis from its origin as a fur trading post to its development as a center of commerce. Tours are available, or you may want to wander on your own, exploring a building that survived and exemplifies the tumultuous years of our nation's history.

COMMONLY ASKED QUESTIONS

How many people visit the JNEM each year?
Park visitation averages over 2 1/2 million people annually.

When are the busiest months?
During the summer months, visitation varies between 15,000 and 30,000 people per day, with just under 6,000 going to the top of the Arch.

How tall is the Arch?
630 feet tall and 630 feet wide. 630 feet = 192 meters.

How heavy is the Arch?
17,246 tons: 886 tons exterior stainless steel plate, 2,157 tons structural steel plate, 1,408 tons steel stiffeners, 368 tons steel reinforcing bars, 300 tons interior steel members, stairs and tram systems, plus 12,127 tons concrete.

How many individual sections make up the Arch?
142 sections, 71 in each leg, there is no center piece.

What is the projected life span of the Arch?
1,000 years, beginning in 1965.

Did anyone lose his life during construction of the Arch?
Fortunately, there were no fatalities. 13 were anticipated.

When was the Arch started and completed?
Ground breaking for the Memorial: June 23, 1959. Excavation of the Visitor Center began: February 11, 1961. First section placed: February 12, 1963. The last section placed: October 28, 1965. Inside work completed and monument dedicated on: May 25, 1968.

How did workers reach their work site over 500 feet in the air?
An elevator on the outside of each leg, completely automatic, traveled about 100 feet per minute. Mechanisms were installed to compensate for the changing curvature.

How long does the tram ride take?
4 minutes up, 3 minutes down.

Why don't the tram cars turn upside down?
Capsules are designed to rotate. A special motor helps to keep the capsule upright.

How many steps are in the Arch? Why can't we walk down?
For maintenance, there is an elevator in the lower half of the legs as well as a spiral staircase of 1,076 steps and 105 landings. Visitors must use the trams due to extreme temperature conditions in the stairwell and other hazards.

Does the Arch sway in the wind?
Top sways between 1/2″ and 1″ in a 20 mph wind. It was designed to withstand a 150 mph wind, which would only cause the Arch to sway 18 inches in an east-west direction.

Does the Arch ever get struck by lightning?
Yes, but with little effect. There are lightning rods on top, and there is an extensive copper cable system embedded in the ground below the Arch.

Who funded the building of the Arch?
Both the federal government and the city of St. Louis supplied the $30 million needed for construction.

How could the engineers be sure the two legs would meet at the top?
All calculations were carried out to 5 decimal places for accuracy. The geometry control readings were taken at night since the sun caused the legs to expand. The margin of error was 1/64 of an inch.

Is this really a National Park?
Yes, Jefferson National Expansion Memorial is a National Historic Site, a unit of the National Park Service. JNEM is one of the urban parks in the service.

More Exciting Gateway Arch Products

To order call 1-800-537-7962

toll-free 7 days a week
In Missouri call: 314-231-5474
24 hour Fax: 314-231-7424

Or use the card below, but be sure to enclose in envelope with payment or credit card information and mail to: Gone West, 11 N. 4th Street, St. Louis, MO 63102.

To receive our FREE catalog featuring books and videos about the history of the American West, complete the postage-paid card and mail today or call 1-800-537-7962!

13305 Video: Monument to the Dream: The Construction of the Gateway Arch
Color VHS- *$19.95*
The Gateway Arch is a beautiful historic monument dedicated to the early pioneers who developed the West and to the citizens who have contributed to the greatness of this country. In *Monument to the Dream*, viewers will be fascinated as they re-live the construction of this great memorial from beginning to end. 30 minutes.

22750 Video: Touring the Gateway Arch: Behind the Scenes at a National Memorial
Color VHS- *$19.95*
The Gateway Arch beautifully symbolizes the pioneering spirit of those who opened and settled the land west of the Mississippi during the 1800s. Through original construction footage, you'll see how the Arch was constructed and understand why it came about. We'll take you on a tram ride to the top, explore the Museum of Westward Expansion, tour the historic Old Courthouse, and stroll the park grounds. 30 minutes.

Narrated by **Bob Costas**

19508 Audio Book: Story of the Gateway Arch (on one cassette) *$8.95*
A great addition to this book and a wonderful companion while traveling!

Narrated by **Joseph Campanella**

2320 The Building of the Arch *$6.95*
This newly revised pictorial history of the building of the Gateway Arch includes historic photographs taken during the construction, contemporary photographs, and narrative text describing the construction. 28 pg. paperback.

☐ **Yes,** send me the latest *Gone West!*® catalog!

NAME _____

STREET ADDRESS (NO POST OFFICE BOXES) _____

CITY _____ STATE ____ ZIP __/__/__

( ) _____
DAYTIME PHONE NUMBER   TODAY'S DATE

How would you like to pay for your order?

☐ Personal check to: Gone West!
☐ MasterCard   ☐ Discover
☐ Visa   ☐ Am Ex/Optima

Enter credit Card number here:
☐☐☐☐☐☐☐☐☐☐☐☐☐☐☐☐

Expiration date ☐/☐

_____
Signature of card holder

ITEM #	TITLE– DESCRIPTION	QTY	PRICE	TOTAL
13305	Monument to the Dream		$19.95	
22750	Touring the Gateway Arch		$19.95	
19508	Audio Book: Story of the Gateway Arch		$8.95	
2320	The Building of the Arch		$6.95	

SHIPPING &HANDLING	EXPRESS SERVICE	
ORDER SUBTOTAL:	FIND GROUND SHIPPING AT LEFT THEN ADD:	**SUBTOTAL**
UP TO $25.... $4.50		
$25.01– $50.... $5.50	$10 MORE FOR TWO DAY	**SHIPPING & HANDLING**
$50.01– $75.... $6.50	$15 MORE FOR NEXT DAY	Add shipping for next day/2nd day
$75.01–$100.... $7.50		
OVER $100.... $7.50 + $.50 per item		**TOTAL**

Enclose all merchandise orders in an envelope with check or credit card information.

Jefferson National Expansion Historical Association

JNEHA is an educational, not-for-profit organization supporting the interpretive and educational programs of the National Park Service. Based in St. Louis, Missouri, JNEHA was established in 1961 and is located at the Gateway Arch, part of the 91-acre Jefferson National Expansion Memorial. The purposes of JNEHA, as set forth in its charter, include public education about the history of the westward expansion begun by Thomas Jefferson. Donations to JNEHA help develop and maintain quality visitor programs which emphasize the preservation and historic significance of the westward movement.